Henry Lord Middle School

WORLD IN
FOCUS

FOCUS ON
NIGERIA

ALI BROWNLIE BOJANG AND ROB BOWDEN

WORLD ALMANAC® LIBRARY

Please visit our web site at: www.worldalmanaclibrary.com
For a free color catalog describing World Almanac® Library's list of high-quality books
and multimedia programs, call 1-800-848-2928 (USA) or 1-800-387-3178 (Canada).
World Almanac® Library's fax: (414) 332-3567.

Library of Congress Cataloging-in-Publication Data available upon request from publisher.
Fax (414) 336-0157 for the attention of the Publishing Records Department.

ISBN 0-8368-6220-1 (lib. bdg.)
ISBN 0-8368-6239-2 (softcover)

This North American edition first published in 2006 by
World Almanac® Library
A Member of the WRC Media Family of Companies
330 West Olive Street, Suite 100
Milwaukee, WI 53212 USA

Commissioning editor: Victoria Brooker
Editor: Kelly Davis
Inside design: Chris Halls, www.mindseyedesign.co.uk
Cover design: Hodder Wayland
Series concept and project management by EASI-Educational Resourcing (info@easi-er.co.uk)
Statistical research: Anna Bowden

World Almanac® Library editor: Alan Wachtel
World Almanac® Library cover design: Scott Krall

Population Density Map © 2003 UT-Battelle, LLC. All rights reserved.
Data for population density maps reproduced under licence from UT-Battelle, LLC.
All rights reserved.
Maps and graphs: Martin Darlison, Encompass Graphics

Picture acknowledgements:
The author and publisher would like to thank the following for allowing their pictures to be
reproduced in this publication:
Corbis 10 and 25 (Reuters/George Esiri), 12 and 13 (Bettmann), 34 (Reuters/Mike Segar), 35
(Reuters/Finbarr O'Reilly), 36 (Reuters/Jason Reed); EASI-Images/Roy Maconachie 1, 8, 14, 20, 28,
33, 39, 43, 46, 48, 55, 57 and 59; EASI-Images/Lorena Ros 5, 6, 9, 11, 15, 16, 17, 19, 21, 22, 23, 24,
26, 27, 29, 30, 31, 32, 37, 38, 40, 41, 42, 44, 45, 47, 49(t), 49(b), 50, 51, 52, 53, 54, 56 and 58.

The directional arrow portrayed on the map on page 7 provides only an approximation of north.
The data used to produce the graphics and data panels in this title were the latest available at the
time of production.

Printed in China

1 2 3 4 5 6 7 8 9 10 09 08 07 06

CONTENTS

Cover: Beautiful traditional attire is worn by these young women and girls at a village celebration.

Title page: These Nigerian women, photographed at an outdoor market, wear clothing that combines traditional and contemporary styles.

CHAPTER 1

Nigeria – An Overview

Nigeria is the most populous country in Africa and also one of the most powerful countries on the continent. It is sometimes called the "Giant of Africa." When many people think of Nigeria, they often imagine a country that is chaotic, dirty, and noisy, with a reputation for crime and corruption. Although these are very real problems that affect large parts of the country, there is much more to Nigeria. It boasts, for example, one of the richest and most complex cultures in Africa, thanks to the extraordinary diversity of its population, which consists of over 250 ethnic groups and speakers of more than four hundred languages. Nigeria's three main religions—Christianity, Islam, and traditional beliefs—add to this cultural diversity. Islam, in particular, has had a significant and controversial impact in northern Nigeria, where it is an important influence on everyday life. For example, sharia, or Islamic law, has been adopted in several of the country's northern states. In spite of the differences among Nigerians, many of them share important aspects of their culture—especially the value they place on family life and extended family networks and the importance they give to ceremonies and social events.

? Did You Know?

The flag of Nigeria uses green to symbolize the land and fertility and white to symbolize peace and unity.

A WASTED OPPORTUNITY?

The discovery of oil in Nigeria in the 1950s brought great hope to the country's people. Other countries around the world had seen rapid improvements in their standard of living following the discovery of oil, one of the most valued natural resources. Nigerians felt further optimism when their country gained its independence from Britain in 1960, ending almost one hundred years of colonial rule. Unfortunately, their hopes were short-lived. Successive Nigerian governments—most of them military-controlled—mismanaged the country's oil revenues. Far from benefiting from the newfound oil wealth, most Nigerians have experienced drops in both their standards of living and their incomes.

The misuse of oil revenues and the failed hopes of millions of Nigerians have been sources of great tension and unrest in the country. Almost since it gained independence, Nigeria has been disturbed by civil unrest as different groups have competed for power and access to land and resources. Because these competing groups have usually had strong ethnic and religious identities, the unrest and tensions in the country have gone far beyond politics and have become part of everyday life.

▶ Young girls in traditional Nigerian dress. Although Nigeria has seen many changes in the last few decades, certain customs and traditions, such as the way the birth of a child is celebrated and the type of food people eat, remain strong.

A NEW BEGINNING

In 1999, after almost three decades of military rule, Nigeria returned to civilian, democratic government. Despite the many hardships still faced by Nigerians, people in the country remain optimistic that this change in government was the beginning of a new era of democracy and freedom. Nigeria still has a good chance of becoming a prosperous country in which the majority of Nigerians benefit from their nation's riches. The country's vast oil reserves give it global strategic importance. Nigeria is also rich in other natural resources, many of which are underexploited or not exploited at all.

The country has new opportunities, too, such as a share in the global tourist industry—the world's fastest-growing industry. Nigeria

possesses tropical forests, deserts, and beautiful beaches. Its long history, spanning several different civilizations, has also left it with a legacy of exceptionally beautiful arts and crafts and ancient walled cities and villages, many of which have barely changed in thousands of years. These features could help to make Nigeria an attractive tourist destination. The first challenge for Nigeria, however, is to overcome the damage inflicted on the country in the past by corrupt military regimes. With the return of democratic government, foreign investors are slowly coming back, and during 2004, the economy improved. But, at the start of the twenty-first century, Nigeria still has a long way to go before meeting the unrealized ambitions of its ever-optimistic people.

Physical Geography Data

- Land area: 351,648 square miles/ 910,768 square kilometers
- Water area: 5,019 sq miles/13,000 sq km
- Total area: 356,667 sq miles/ 923,768 sq km
- World rank by area: 32
- Land boundaries: 2,513 miles/ 4,043 kilometers
- Border countries: Benin, Cameroon, Chad, Niger
- Coastline: 530 miles/853 km
- Highest point: Chappal Waddi (7,936 feet/2,419 meters)
- Lowest point: Atlantic Ocean (0 m/0 ft)

Source: CIA World Factbook

▼ Nigeria has the second-largest economy in Africa. It includes major businesses, many of which are related to oil, and hundreds of smaller local businesses providing for local needs.

? Did You Know?

In 2005, 14.6 percent of all Africans— about one out of seven—was a Nigerian.

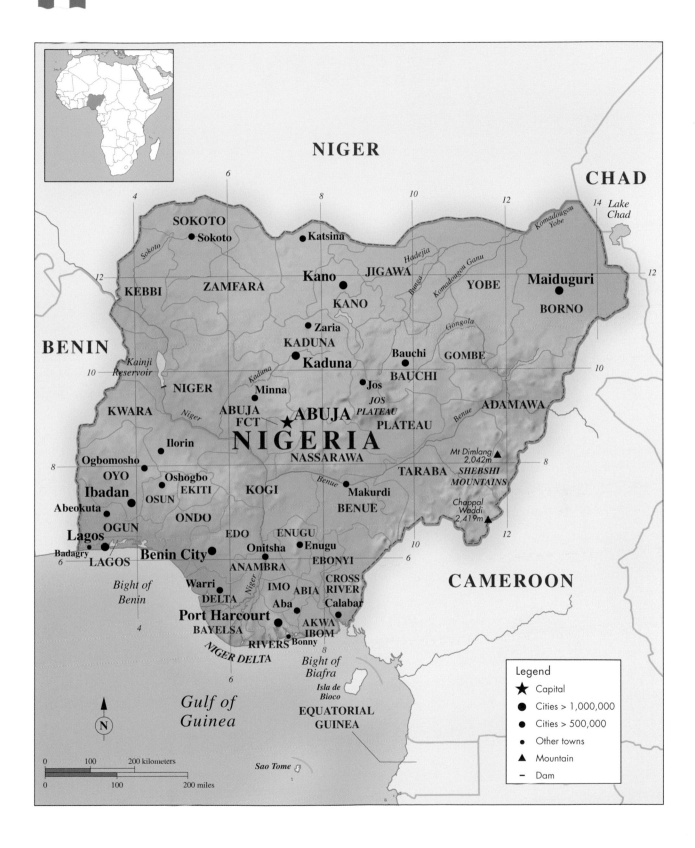

NIGER

CHAD

Lake
Chad

SOKOTO
● Sokoto
● Katsina

KEBBI
ZAMFARA
JIGAWA
Kano
●
KANO
Zaria
●
YOBE
Maiduguri
BORNO

BENIN

Kainji
Reservoir
NIGER
KWARA

Kaduna
KADUNA
●
Bauchi
●
GOMBE
BAUCHI
Minna
●
Jos
●
JOS
PLATEAU
ABUJA
FCT
★ ABUJA
PLATEAU
ADAMAWA

NIGERIA
NASSARAWA
Mt Dimlang ▲
2,042m
SHEBSHI
MOUNTAINS

Ilorin
●
Ogbomosho
●
OYO
Oshogbo
●
EKITI
KOGI
Benue
Makurdi
●
TARABA
Chappal
Waddi
2,419m ▲

Ibadan
●
OSUN
ONDO
BENUE

Abeokuta
●
Lagos
●
OGUN
EDO
ENUGU
Onitsha
● Enugu
●

Badagry
●
LAGOS
Benin City
●
ANAMBRA
EBONYI

CAMEROON

Bight of
Benin
Warri
●
DELTA
IMO
ABIA
CROSS
RIVER
Calabar
●

Port Harcourt
●
BAYELSA
Aba
●
AKWA
IBOM

RIVERS
Bonny
●

NIGER DELTA

Bight of
Biafra

Isla de
Bioco

Gulf of
Guinea

EQUATORIAL
GUINEA

N

Sao Tome

0   100   200 kilometers
0   100   200 miles

Legend
★ Capital
● Cities > 1,000,000
● Cities > 500,000
• Other towns
▲ Mountain
– Dam

CHAPTER 2

History

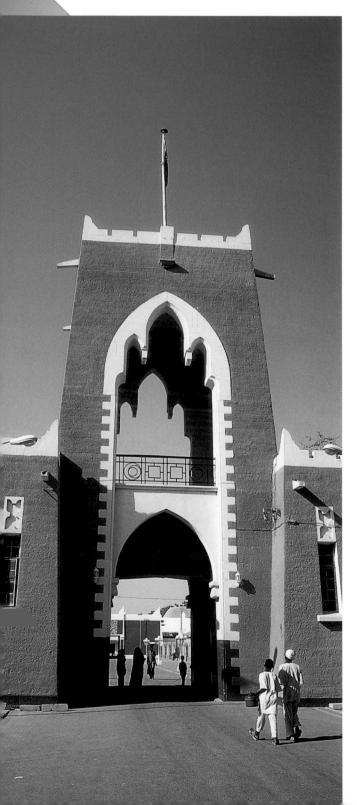

People have lived in the region now known as Nigeria for at least eleven thousand years, and much of Nigeria's early history is the separate histories of its different ethnic groups. The earliest evidence of human inhabitants in the region is a skeleton found in southwestern Nigeria dating from about 9000 B.C. Other remains show that, about four thousand years ago, Nigeria was sparsely populated with people who grew crops and kept cattle, goats, and sheep. The first society in Nigeria was the Nok culture, which flourished on the Jos Plateau between around 500 B.C. and A.D. 200. The Nok made fine terracotta figurines and probably knew how to work tin and iron.

EMPIRES AND CITY-STATES

Later, between the eighth and nineteenth centuries, several empires and city-states flourished and declined across the region that is modern-day Nigeria. The kingdom of Kanem was the earliest, emerging to the east of Lake Chad some time before A.D. 900. Traders were drawn to the lake for rest and water as they traveled from North Africa across the Sahara desert. The traders brought Islam to the region, and by the eleventh century, the Kanem rulers had all become Muslims. The kingdom of Kanem lost much of its power during the twelfth century but re-emerged to the west of Lake Chad as the Kanem-Bornu empire in the late sixteenth century, following a merger with the Bornu rulers of central Sudan.

◀ The city gates of Kano are one of Nigeria's most important historical structures. They are a reminder of the former power of the great city-states.

The Kanem-Bornu empire extended its influence as far west as Hausaland in modern-day northern and north-central Nigeria. The Hausa are thought to have occupied this area since about the sixth century, and they formed a number of centralized city-states, each of which had grand city walls and a central market. An emir, or ruler, controlled each state through a number of chiefs, who, in turn, controlled surrounding villages and collected taxes. Kano, Katsina, and Zaria are modern Nigerian cities that began as Hausa city-states.

City-states were also found in southern Nigeria, where several powerful Yoruba kingdoms vied for power. The first Yoruba city-state was established in about the eleventh century at Ife in southwestern Nigeria. Benin, Oyo, and Ilorin emerged a little later. Between these city-states, they controlled the area from the Niger River, to the east, and Togo (now an independent country), to the west. The city-states were at their peak in the fifteenth century and became famous for their exquisite ivory, brass, and bronze artworks. The Benin kingdom, in particular, left a legacy of beautiful bronze sculpture that are known as the Benin Bronzes.

Nigeria's Hausa and Yoruba city-states lost many of their powers after 1804 when Usman Dan Fodio, a Muslim scholar from the Fulani people (a mainly pastoral group from northern Nigeria), launched a series of holy wars, or jihads. These wars displaced many of the emirs and created the new caliphate of Sokoto. In south-western Nigeria, the collapse of Oyo led to the Yoruba wars, which lasted until 1886.

▶ A replica of a Benin Bronze. Many of the best original Benin Bronzes were taken by the British and are today housed in the British Museum in London.

THE IGBO

In the southeast, the Igbo civilization can be traced back to at least A.D. 900. The Igbo lived in small, independent villages, each of which had its own elected council rather than a chief. Although they traded along the coast, the dense rain forest vegetation, in which they lived, kept them isolated from the rest of the region.

THE ARRIVAL OF THE EUROPEANS

In the late fifteenth century, Portuguese traders became the first Europeans to arrive on the Nigerian coast, and they were quickly followed by British, French, and Dutch traders. Traders established links with Benin and Oyo to gain ivory, gold, pepper, and slaves, but northern kingdoms and city-states were left virtually untouched. In spite of Britain's efforts to halt slavery—including by outlawing it in 1807—the slave trade continued. It was a highly profitable business for local leaders and slave traders. British forces replaced those local leaders who supported the slave trade, and they also tried to police the coast to stop the practice. In 1861, Britain annexed Lagos, claiming it as British territory, so that Britain could use it as a port and ensure that it was free of slave trading.

Focus on: The Slave Trade

▲ Local people re-enact the days of slavery in the former slave port town of Badagry, located in southwest Nigeria, in 2002.

From the seventeenth to the nineteenth centuries, European traders established coastal ports to transport slaves to South America and the Caribbean. The southwestern coast of Nigeria became known as the "slave coast." Many people died during violent raids deep into Nigerian territory by merchants looking for slaves. Over 15,000 people were shipped annually from the Bight of Benin and another 15,000 from the Bight of Biafra. In total, up to 30 million slaves may have been sold and transported into slavery from the Nigerian coast. They were sent across the Atlantic Ocean to work on the sugar and cotton plantations of the Caribbean and the southern colonies of North America. Conditions on the ships were poor, and many died on the journeys.

COLONIALISM

At a conference in 1884 in Berlin, Germany, the dominant European powers of the time carved up Africa between them. Britain claimed southern Nigeria from the peoples there, mainly the Yoruba and the Igbo, and established control by making treaties with local leaders. Where they encountered resistance, the British used their superior military power to seize control through force.

In the late nineteenth century, Britain began trading in northern Nigeria and negotiated further treaties with local leaders there. By 1900, Britain had gained sufficient control of the region to declare that Nigeria would be administered as two protectorates—the Protectorate of Southern Nigeria and the Protectorate of Northern Nigeria. In 1914, these were joined, and Nigeria was created, bringing the region's different peoples together as one political entity. Britain imposed a system called "indirect rule," under which local leaders were allowed to rule as long as they collected taxes for Britain and complied with what Britain wanted. This succeeded in the Islamic north, where the emirs acted as executors of British policy, but in southern Yorubaland, resistance was greater.

While under British rule, most of Nigeria's trade was with Britain. Crops such as palm oil, groundnuts, and cotton were produced in large quantities for export to Britain. This focus on exports forced many farmers to change the crops they grew, reducing amounts of those they grew for their own use and damaging their trading links with North Africa and neighboring coastal states.

INDEPENDENCE AND AFTER

After decades of political struggle against colonial rule, Nigeria gained its independence from Britain on October 1, 1960. This resistance was led mainly by Nigerian politicians who had been educated in the West and by journalists such as Nnamdi Azikiwe and Obafemi Awolowo. It was a long, hard fight, but it was bloodless. In contrast, the country's first few years of independence were characterized by many, sometimes violent, conflicts within and between Nigeria's different regions and ethnic groups. For example, in

▲ De Aholu Whenu Menu Toyi I, the oba, or king, of Badagry, influences the workings of government as well as holding a local court. During the colonial period, the British controlled much of Nigeria by making agreements with local obas, who ruled on their behalf.

February 1964, the Tiv people, who wanted to govern themselves, launched an attack against the local authorities, but it was suppressed by the Nigerian federal army. In 1963, Nigeria became a federal republic made up of three regions, each with limited self-government, but the unrest continued. In January 1966, Igbo army officers staged a coup, and the country's first military government was established, only to be overthrown by a Hausa coup in July 1966.

MILITARY RULE

A series of military governments controlled Nigeria from 1966 to 1999, with the exception of a brief period of civilian rule between 1979 and 1983, when Lieutenant-General Olusegun Obasanjo handed power to a democratically elected government. General Sani Abacha, one of the country's later military government leaders, led Nigeria from 1993 until his sudden death in 1998. Abacha's rule was marked by

▼ Supporters cheer after elections held in December 1959 to prepare Nigeria for independence from Britain on October 1, 1960. Abubakar Tafawa Balewa was elected prime minister to lead Nigeria to independence.

serious human rights abuses.

Those who criticized his regime—including journalists and human rights activists—were often imprisoned or killed. After protests from the Nigerian people and pressure from the international community, elections were held in 1999, and civilian rule was restored. Olusegun Obasanjo, a former military government leader, became president of Nigerian's new civilian government in 1999 and was re-elected in 2003.

VIOLENCE

Since independence, Nigeria has regularly experienced violent conflicts: clashes between the federal government and the minority ethnic groups of the oil-rich Niger Delta over oil revenues; disputes over land in the multiethnic Middle Belt (the central region of Nigeria); and clashes between Christian and Muslim communities both in the north of the country and in the Middle Belt.

Focus on: The Biafra War

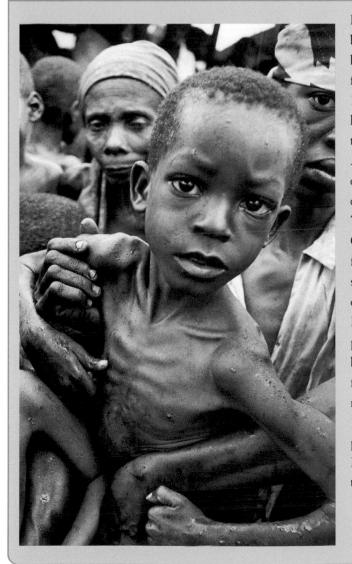

In 1966, the Hausa people of northern Nigeria became especially resentful of the wealthy, better-educated Igbo people, who came mainly from Nigeria's eastern region. In September 1966, the Hausa people's increasing resentment led some of them to massacre up to thirty thousand Igbos living in northern Nigeria. About one million more Igbo fled to the eastern region, and non-Igbo people were expelled from the Igbo's eastern homelands. The governor of the eastern region, Colonel Odumegwu Ojukwu, declared independence from Nigeria in May 1967 and formed the new sovereign state of Biafra. Fighting soon broke out between Nigerian forces and forces from Biafra. The conflict, in which several million people may have died, was one of Africa's bloodiest civil wars. Because the Nigerian forces cut off the supply routes into Biafra, many Biafrans died of starvation. By January 1970, Nigerian military gains and a starving population forced the Biafran leaders into exile. Biafra ceased to exist on January 15, 1970, and the region again became part of Nigeria.

◀ The images of famine in Biafra shocked people all over the world in the late 1960s.

Landscape and Climate

Nigeria covers an area of 356,667 sq miles (923,768 sq km)—slightly more than twice the size of California and three times the size of Britain. It has a wide range of different landscapes, from swamps and deserts to mountains and plains. The country's two main rivers, the Niger and the Benue, meet to the south of the center of Nigeria, forming a "Y" shape.

LANDSCAPE

Washed by the Atlantic Ocean, the southern coast of Nigeria is a low-lying area of sandy beaches, lagoons, and mangrove swamps. To the east, the country's coastline is broken by the huge delta of the Niger River. The coastal plain, with its sedimentary rocks, extends about 6 miles (10 km) inland, from where a tract of rain forest gradually rises toward the Middle Belt. In eastern Nigeria, on the country's border with Cameroon, lies the Central Highlands and Chappal Waddi, Nigeria's highest point at 7,936 feet (2,419 m).

▼ Rain-forest vegetation once covered much of southern Nigeria, but today it is only found in a few areas, such as part of the state of Cross River.

Nigeria's Middle Belt, which lies north of the coastal plain, has an average altitude of about 2,000 feet (700 m). Isolated areas on the Jos Plateau reach 3,900 feet (1,200 m). The Jos Plateau is part of the Central Plateau, an area of savannah grasslands and open woodland. The Central Plateau has a few isolated areas of volcanic rocks that form dramatic, beautiful scenery with waterfalls and rock pools.

The northern half of Nigeria is made up of ancient crystalline rocks that have been weathered and eroded over millions of years, forming broad, level plateaus with low granite hills, or inselbergs. From these plateau lands, the altitude falls to the low-lying Chad and Sokoto basins in the country's far northeast and northwest. The northernmost part of this area is mainly desert and semidesert and marks the southern edge of the Sahara Desert.

▲ A villager passes along a path that crosses the granite hills, or inselbergs, that are typical of the Jos Plateau area around the city of Jos.

CLIMATE

Nigeria's climate is equatorial in the south, tropical in the center, and semiarid in the north. Temperatures are generally high all year round, usually over 86 °Fahrenheit (30 °Celsius), with the highest temperatures toward the end of the dry season. The main climatic variable for the whole country is rainfall, which is controlled by two air masses. Moist, northward-moving, maritime air comes from the Atlantic Ocean, and dry, continental air moves south from the Sahara Desert. These air currents meet in the Inter-Tropical Convergence Zone (ITCZ). Their seasonal movement dictates Nigeria's and, indeed, much of Africa's, rainfall pattern.

▲ These men are fishing in one of the mangrove creeks of the Niger Delta.

Southern Nigeria, with its equatorial climate, is hot and rainy most of the year, with a relatively dry period between November and March. The rainy season usually begins in February as moist Atlantic air arrives. The highest rainfall is along the southeastern coast, particularly around Bonny, where average annual rainfall is more than 157 inches (400 centimeters). Most of the southeast receives 79 to 118 inches (200 to 300 cm) of rain a year. In the southwest, a rainfall decrease in August allows a period for grain to be harvested.

Focus on: The Niger Delta

The Niger Delta protrudes into the Gulf of Guinea. It covers an area of approximately 5,600 sq miles (14,500 sq km) and is made up of swampland, intricate networks of creeks and lagoons, mangroves, and numerous small islands. It drains an area of more than 380,000 square miles (984,200 sq km) and is one of the largest delta systems in the world. Oil formed in this region millions of years ago from the fossils of tiny sea creatures and plants that accumulated on the seabed. The Niger Delta is the home of many different ethnic groups and has been extensively exploited for its oil.

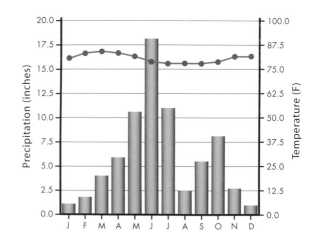

▲ Average monthly climate conditions in Lagos

Nigeria's central and northern areas have a tropical climate. The far north is semiarid. These regions have two main seasons—the long dry season from October to May and the short rainy season from June to September. The rains can be heavy and frequently result in flash floods. The north, which is drier than the south, can have five months with no rain.

The greatest extremes of temperature in Nigeria are found in the northeast. In this area, temperatures often reach as high as 111 °F (44 °C) before the onset of the rains and can drop as low as 43 °F (6 °C) during the occasional intrusion of cool air from the north between December and February.

In the dry season, Nigeria's sky is often laden with sand and dust from the Sahara brought in by the northeast trade winds, which are known as the Harmattan. These winds can be felt as far south as Lagos.

? Did You Know?

In June 2002, more than sixty people died of heatstroke in the northeastern city of Maiduguri when temperatures reached 131 °F (55 °C).

Focus on: Climate Change

Frequent droughts occurred in Nigeria during the 1970s and 1980s, particularly in the north, leading to crop failure and famine. Experts consider it to have been one of the driest periods in centuries, and they have speculated that the dryness might be a sign of climate change. Because the Nigerian government wants to reduce the potential impact of climate change, it has recently announced measures to stop the flaring, or burning, of natural gas in the oil fields of the Niger Delta by 2008. Gas flaring produces large quantities of carbon dioxide and methane—two of the gases that have been linked to the process of climate change. Gas vapors are a by-product of oil drilling, and they are flared in order to dispose of them. In 2003, Nigeria was the site of about 12.5 percent of the world's gas flaring.

▼ Gas flaring from an oil well in the Niger Delta region. Some people think gas flaring may contribute to climate change.

CHAPTER 4

Population and Settlements

In 2005, Nigeria had about 130 million people, making it by far the most heavily populated country in Africa. Nigeria also has one of the fastest-growing populations in Africa—and, indeed, in the world. From 2000 to 2005, its annual population growth rate was 2.5 percent, compared to an average in Africa of 2.2 percent a year and an average around the world of 1.2 percent a year. Experts predict that population growth will begin to slow in Nigeria, but it is still expected to grow by about 2.3 percent each year for the years from 2000 to 2015.

Children are highly valued in Nigerian society because most parents believe that their children will look after them when they are elderly, an important consideration in a country that has limited social welfare services. As a result, Nigerian families are generally very large.

The average Nigerian woman gives birth about five times in her lifetime, although women who are better educated tend to have fewer children.

Nigeria's level of growth is unsustainable both for the country and for its individual families, many of whom live in poverty. The country's population growth has severe consequences for the quality of life of all Nigerians because it puts a huge strain on the country's services, including water supplies, housing, health care, and education.

With poverty and a lack of basic health care comes a high infant mortality rate. In 2003, for every 1,000 children born, 133 died before reaching the age of five, and life expectancy at

Population Data

- Population: 127.1 million
- Population 0–14 yrs: 43%
- Population 15–64 yrs: 54%
- Population 65+ yrs: 3%
- Population growth rate (2000–2005): 2.5%
- Population density: 356.4 per sq mile/ 137.6 per sq km
- Urban population: 47%
- Major cities: Lagos 11,135,000; Kano 2,884,000; Ibadan 2,375,000

Sources: United Nations and World Bank

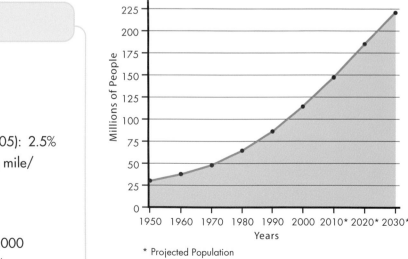

* Projected Population

▲ Population growth, 1950–2030

▲ Over 40 percent of Nigeria's population is under fourteen years old.

birth was just 51.1 years for men and 51.8 years for women. Another factor that is having an increasing impact on Nigeria's population is HIV/AIDS. By 2003, it was estimated that 4.6 percent of men and 6.2 percent of women between the ages of fifteen and forty-nine were living with HIV/AIDS. Some health experts believe this already-high proportion could double by the year 2010.

? Did You Know?

In 2004, Nigeria was the tenth most heavily populated country in the world.

Focus on: The Census

Although the size of Nigeria's population can be estimated, its precise size is hard to determine. A census was held in the country in 1991, but the results were contested by rival regions and ethnic groups. The problem is that whichever ethnic group turns out to be the largest ends up with a greater share of power in government because seats in the House of Representatives are allocated on the basis of population size. Because of this policy, taking a census is very controversial. The government frequently puts it off, saying that it could cause conflict and violence. If it were found that the leaders were not from the dominant group, the census result could challenge their position of power. A new census is proposed for 2005.

POPULATION DENSITY

Nigeria had an average population density in 2005 of 365 people per square mile (141 people per sq km), but distribution of people is not even throughout the country. The south is more densely populated, with 200 to 400 people per square mile (500 to 1,000 per square km). In semiarid parts of the north, population density is often very low, but high concentrations of people live in and around urban areas such as Kano and Sokoto.

MIGRATION TO THE CITIES

Rural poverty and a lack of job opportunities have forced many young people to move to the cities. It is fairly common to find villages where most of the young, able-bodied men have gone to the cities, leaving women to do the farming and take care of the children and elderly. In some cases, this migration has led to the complete abandonment of farms.

Nigeria has experienced rapid urbanization, with 48.3 percent of its population living in towns and cities as of 2005, up from just 15.2 percent in 1960. The urban population is expected to continue increasing to reach about 65 percent of the total population by 2030. Most urban centers in Nigeria are small to medium in size, with only seven having a population of over 750,000 in 2005. Whatever their size, most have grown at

▼ This Hausa/Fulani homestead is in northern Nigeria, which is more sparsely populated and more rural than the country's southern regions.

an extraordinary rate, with little urban planning. This growth has resulted in massive problems that present considerable health risks, including traffic congestion, poor housing, inadequate waste management, and inadequate water supplies. Air pollution caused by the burning of waste, the use of wood and charcoal for cooking, and the emissions from poor-quality vehicles on crowded roads is also a problem.

▲ This dense urban area in Kano, Nigeria's second-largest city, consists mostly of low-quality housing and is typical of Nigeria's urban centers.

? Did You Know?

Nigeria covers 15 percent of the land area of West Africa but has 56 percent of its people.

Focus on: Lagos

When Nigeria won its independence in 1960, the city of Lagos, which was then its capital, had a population of just 762,000. By 2005, Lagos's population has grown to about 11.1 million, making it the seventeenth most populous city in the world and one of only twenty megacities, or cities with over 10 million people. By 2015, the United Nations predicts that Lagos's population will top seventeen million, and Lagos will rank ninth among the world's most populous cities. Besides being by far Nigeria's largest city, Lagos is also its leading port and an important center of

intellectual and cultural life, with several universities and colleges, the National Library, and the National Museum. Lagos, however, compares badly with cities in other parts of the world in terms of quality of life, with many of its houses being no more than makeshift huts on unpaved roads with no services. The city does, however, have pockets of good housing and apartment buildings where its wealthy people and the majority of its expatriate community live. Homes in these areas of Lagos have become fortresses in order to guard against crime.

CHAPTER 5

Government and Politics

Nigeria gained its independence in 1960, but the country has been in political turmoil almost ever since then, with its numerous military governments oppressing—and sometimes assassinating—their political rivals. Since its 1999 return to democratic civilian rule, however, the country's government has become much more stable, and many Nigerians are optimistic about the future.

NIGERIA'S FEDERAL SYSTEM

Nigeria became a federal republic in 1963, and it is today made up of thirty-six states and the federal capital territory of Abuja. National laws and decisions on issues such as defense and foreign affairs are made by the central government, while each state has a large degree of autonomy and can make state laws. In northern Nigeria, several predominantly Islamic states have adopted sharia, or Islamic law, as their state legal system.

Nigeria's president leads a parliament. Its upper chamber, called the Senate, contains 109 seats, three for each of Nigeria's 36 states and one for the federal capital territory. Its lower chamber, or the House of Representatives, contains 360 seats, with 10 seats for each state. The country's president and members of both chambers of parliament are elected for four-year terms.

The federal system allows Nigeria's diverse ethnic and religious groups to be governed according to the laws and principles of their own cultures. To some extent, the federal system also helps balance the power between the country's leading ethnic groups—the Hausa and Fulani in the north, the Yoruba in the southwest, and the Igbo in the southeast.

◀ Pictures of President Olusegun Obasanjo appears on posters all around Nigeria.

The Nigerian federal system does not always run smoothly, however, and disputes between the central government and individual states are common, particularly over the allocation of national resources.

▼ This picture shows a meeting of the chiefs of Badagry. These chiefs are traditional governors who still make decisions on many local issues.

MOVING THE CAPITAL

Until 1976, the mainly Yoruba city of Lagos, in southern Nigeria, was the country's capital. In that year, the capital was moved to the new city of Abuja, located just north of the point at which the Niger and Benue Rivers meet and almost in the center of the country. It was thought that the relocation of the capital to a place between the main north and south ethnic regions would help balance political power and calm the tensions between the regions.

RETURN TO CIVILIAN RULE

After years of condemnation by the international community for the country's lack of democracy and its disregard for human rights, the country's military leader, General Abdulsalam Abubakar, voluntarily stepped down in 1999, and Nigeria returned to civilian rule and democracy. A new constitution was also adopted in 1999, guaranteeing Nigerians freedom of expression and religion and prohibiting discrimination on grounds of ethnicity, religion, gender, or place of origin. With the introduction of these reforms, sanctions that had previously been imposed on Nigeria by the international community were dropped. Nigeria has managed to maintain a democratic civilian government into the early twenty-first century, but allegations of corruption and problems caused by the slow pace of change still plague its political leaders. The international community, however, continues to support the country's transition to civilian rule, hoping to prevent a return to Nigeria's turbulent past. In February 2005, for example, the European Union pledged funds to help Nigeria conduct a full population census—the first since its return to

Focus on: Controversy over Sharia

Nigeria's national legal system is based on the English system, but in 2000, a number of largely Muslim states in the north of the country adopted sharia, or Islamic law. Sharia is used in both civil and criminal cases, but its laws sometimes conflict with federal laws, as in the case of Amina Lawal. In 2002, the Sharia court of Katsina State sentenced Lawal to be stoned to death for having given birth outside of marriage. This sentence was much harsher than any that would have been given under the federal law and sparked protests both within and beyond Nigeria. The Sharia Court of Appeal later quashed the sentence and Amina Lawal was released, but her case highlighted the controversy over the acceptance of sharia in the northern regions of Nigeria. Although sharia does not apply to non-Muslims, many non-Muslims living in the north object to it

▲ Amina Lawal with her baby and her father.

being adopted as a legal system in their states. There have been several violent clashes between Muslims and non-Muslims since the sharia system has been adopted in Nigeria's northern states. In total, more than ten thousand people have died in these violent confrontations.

democracy. The results of this census will help the government to better plan the development of the country.

UNREST CONTINUES

Return to civilian rule and the lifting of sanctions have not stopped unrest and violent demonstrations in Nigeria. The people of the Niger Delta, for example, protest against oil companies they claim are damaging their environment and also say that very little of the money earned from oil is used to benefit Delta communities. Government corruption at all levels also remains widespread in Nigeria and undermines people's faith in the democratic process. Holding office in the government is seen by many as a way for individuals to benefit themselves or members of their families, while the problems of growing poverty and poor infrastructure continue for the majority.

Focus on: Nigeria's Human Rights Record

Since the death of General Abacha in June 1998, Nigeria's human rights record has improved considerably. Military decrees allowing people to be detained and put on trial for no apparent reason have been revoked. Prison conditions, however, are still very poor, and corruption, particularly at high levels, continues to be a big problem. Democracy may have been restored, but human rights violations such as police torture and corruption in the judiciary still exist in Nigeria. Even today, the Nigerian government does not easily tolerate those who criticize it. In May 2004, for example, Nigerian novelist Wole Soyinka was arrested after taking part in a demonstration against the government because he believed that the government had failed to restore civil rights quickly enough after the country had returned to civilian rule.

▶ Wole Soyinka speaks about the problem of violence in Nigeria in 2002. As a particularly outspoken Nigerian, he has frequently found himself in trouble with the authorities.

Energy and Resources

Nigeria has mineral resources, such as iron ore, and energy resources, including oil and natural gas. Land and water are also important resources, with about half Nigeria's land suitable for farming or grazing, and lakes, rivers, and streams providing abundant fish.

▼ Even though Nigeria is a major oil producer, fuel is scarce and expensive, and people in the country often have to buy it on the black market from roadside sellers like the ones shown here.

ENERGY SOURCES

Ever since its discovery in the 1950s, Nigeria's oil has been at the heart of the country's politics and economy. In 2003, Nigeria was the world's twelfth-biggest oil producer, providing 2.9 percent of the world's oil. Most of Nigeria's oil is found in the shallow waters of the Niger Delta, but offshore deposits have also been discovered and deep-sea fields are being explored. Nigeria has five government-controlled oil refineries, but they do not produce enough refined oil to meet the country's needs, so about U.S. $2 billion worth of refined oil is imported each year. In August 2004, the Nigerian government announced that all companies producing oil in Nigeria would have to refine at least 50 percent of it within Nigeria by 2006. This will provide new jobs and reduce the need for Nigeria to import refined oil products.

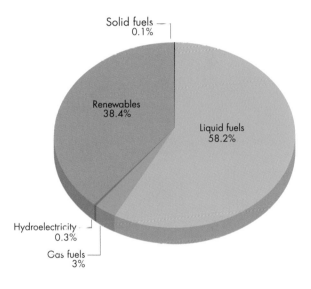

▲ A tanker carrying liquid natural gas (LNG). LNG is a valuable addition to Nigeria's fuel portfolio because it is in growing demand all over the world.

Vast natural gas reserves—estimated at 176.5 trillion cubic feet (5 trillion cubic meters) in 2003, or 2.8 percent of the world's total—have been found in the Niger Delta region. They are only being partly exploited because of a lack of investment. Not surprisingly, foreign investors have been unwilling to invest in Nigeria's gas industry until they are sure of the country's stability. Between 1999 and 2003, however, natural gas production in Nigeria more than tripled, showing that the new government was building confidence. In addition, Nigeria's government is eager to end the wasteful practice of flaring, or burning natural gas produced as a by-product of oil extraction. There are plans to convert this waste gas into liquid natural gas (LNG) for domestic use and export and to construct a West African Gas Pipeline to supply Nigerian gas to Benin, Togo, and Ghana.

ENERGY USE

Between 1980 and 2001, Nigeria's annual energy consumption more than doubled, and it is currently increasing by 15 to 20 percent a year. In relation to other major African nations, however, energy consumption remains low in

Solid fuels
0.1%

Renewables
38.4%

Liquid fuels
58.2%

Hydroelectricity
0.3%

Gas fuels
3%

▲ Energy use by type

Energy Data

- Energy consumption as % of world total: 1.2
- Energy consumption by sector (% of total)
  Industry: 11; Transportation: 7;
  Agriculture: 0; Services: 1; Residential: 81
- CO_2 emissions as % of world total: 0.2
- CO_2 emissions per capita in tons per year: 0.33

Source: World Resources Institute

Nigeria, at less than half that of Egypt and less than a quarter that of South Africa. One reason for Nigeria's low energy consumption is that, by 2004, only about 40 percent of Nigerians had access to electricity.

Nigeria has eight electricity generating stations throughout the country, including five thermal power stations that use oil and gas and three

▲ Like many Nigerians, this young boy regularly gathers wood for use as fuel.

hydroelectric power (HEP) plants, located at Kainji, Jebba, and Shiroro. Electricity generated in Nigeria by HEP has more than doubled since 1980, but because of the country's unreliable rainfall, reservoir levels frequently fall, causing disruptive power outages. Nigeria's government, nevertheless, intends to increase production of HEP. In 2003, it approved the construction of a U.S. $6 billion HEP project on the Mambila Plateau in northeast Nigeria. This plant will produce 3,960 megawatts when completed, a significant percentage of Nigeria's 2004 total electricity capacity of 5,900 megawatts.

Focus on: Biofuels

Despite living in a country rich in fossil fuels, most Nigerians use biofuels such as charcoal, wood, dried vegetation, and wastepaper as their main energy sources. In 2001, biofuels accounted for about 78 percent of the country's energy use. In principle, the use of biofuels is sustainable if the trees from which they come are replanted faster than they are cut down.

? Did You Know?

If Nigeria continues to produce oil at current rates, it has enough proven reserves to keep producing until about 2050.

MINERAL RESOURCES

Nigeria's mineral deposits include iron ore, coal, tin, limestone, gypsum, bauxite, lead, titanium, marble, gold, zinc, and columbite, which is used in making stainless steel. Limestone, which is used in the iron and steel industry, is found in the valleys of the Niger, Benue, and Sokoto Rivers. Tin and columbite are found on the Jos Plateau.

Much of Nigeria's mineral wealth remains unexploited because of lack of investment. The states of Kogi, Enegu, and Niger, for instance, are thought to possess over 3.3 billion tons (3 billion metric tons) of iron ore deposits, but Nigeria still imports iron ore for use in its steel industry. Bauxite, the main raw material for aluminum, has been found on the Mambila and Jos Plateaus. Nigeria's government hopes to use this resource to develop the country's aluminum industry.

FARMING, FORESTRY, AND FISHING

Nigeria's people still largely depend upon the country's land and waters for their living. Over 60 percent of the population is involved in subsistence agriculture, producing food crops such as sorghum and millet, in the north, and yams and cassava, in the south. Nigeria's main cash crops, or crops grown for export, include cocoa, palm oil, groundnuts, and cotton. Forest products are also exported, although the government now imposes limits on forestry to protect Nigeria's remaining rain forests.

Most of Nigeria's lakes and rivers provide fish for local people or for sale in urban markets, but the country's main sources of fish are Lake Chad and Lake Kainji, in the north, and the Niger Delta, in the south. In most parts of Nigeria, fishing is a small-scale industry in which traditional methods are used. In other parts, however, it is a bigger business, and overfishing is a concern in some areas. Atlantic fisheries provide employment and income for many coastal Nigerians. Their livelihoods are threatened, however, by large, unregulated trawlers—some from other West African countries and some from Japan, Korea, and Spain—that are able to catch huge numbers of fish and, thus, deplete the stocks left for the locals. Nigeria's government has imposed restrictions on trawlers; they are not allowed to fish at depths of less than 65 feet (20 m) or less than 3 miles (5 km) from the shoreline. These regulations, however, are not always respected.

▲ Tin mining on the Jos Plateau is no longer profitable as a business, but many small-scale miners continue to extract tin from the area as a way of boosting their incomes.

CHAPTER 7

Economy and Income

Nigeria traditionally had an agricultural economy. The discovery of oil, and later natural gas, radically changed its economy. In the 1970s, when global oil prices were particularly high, Nigeria had the fastest-

▼ This view of Lagos, with its skyscrapers, shows where much of Nigeria's oil revenue has been spent.

growing economy in Africa. For more than a decade, over U.S. $100 billion of oil revenue poured in. It was more money in less time than any nation in sub-Saharan Africa had ever seen. For a while, Nigeria's economy looked set to grow and grow.

SPEND, SPEND, SPEND

Most of the oil revenue was spent on expensive projects that mainly benefited the country's wealthy elite, such as a vast highway system and more than twenty new universities. Little of the money trickled down to ordinary Nigerians, and few of these projects did anything to relieve the problems of the poor. In spite of Nigeria's apparent wealth, the government took out huge loans to develop its grand projects, believing that unlimited oil revenue would allow it to repay the loans. In the mid-1980s, however, the price of oil plummeted, and Nigeria's economic boom fizzled out. Nigeria was unable to repay its loans, and its debts increased from U.S.$9

billion in 1980 to U.S.$33 billion by 1989. In 2002, Nigeria still owed at least U.S.$28 billion. Unless international organizations and governments cancel this debt, it will increase each year as the interest compounds. Today, money that is needed in Nigeria to provide basic services such as education and health care, including drugs to treat HIV/AIDS, and to build a stronger, more varied economy is used instead for interest payments.

▲ Life is hard in this Ogoni village in the Niger Delta. The Ogoni people suffer from poverty and deprivation and have benefited little from the oil found on their land.

? Did You Know?

In 2002, about 70 percent of Nigerians were living on less than U.S.$1 per day, and 90 percent were surviving on less than U.S.$2.

Focus on: Oil Dependency

Oil and natural gas accounted for 90 to 95 percent of Nigeria's export earnings in 2003. In the past, the country's military rulers failed to diversify its economy, and the country became overdependent on oil and natural gas. In 2003, oil provided 20 percent of Nigeria's gross domestic product (GDP), 90 percent of its foreign exchange earnings, and up to 80 percent of government revenues. Being so dependent on oil has made Nigeria extremely vulnerable to changes in oil prices on the world market. Between 1993 and 2003, for instance, the price of a barrel of Nigerian crude oil varied from a low of U.S.$16.25 to a high of U.S.$28.66. When the

price of oil is low, Nigeria has little to fall back on. By joining the Organization of Petroleum Exporting Countries (OPEC) in 1971, however, Nigeria gained some ability to influence world prices. OPEC members meet regularly to agree on production levels in an attempt to affect world oil supplies and, therefore, prices. OPEC has become less influential in recent years because of the emergence of new non-OPEC oil suppliers such as Russia and China. For this reason, Nigeria can no longer rely on OPEC to protect its oil revenues. Instead, Nigeria needs to find new ways of diversifying its economy and reducing its dependence on oil.

POVERTY AND INEQUALITY

The mismanagement of Nigeria's oil revenue has been widely blamed for the country's high rates of poverty. By 2003, Nigeria's average gross national income (GNI) per person had fallen to just U.S.$320—less than one dollar a day. Inequality is also a problem in the country. In 1997 (the last year for which data was collected), the wealthiest 10 percent of Nigerians had almost 41 percent of Nigeria's income. In contrast, the poorest 10 percent shared just 1.6 percent of the national income.

▼ A pastoralist in northern Nigeria herds his goats. Many Nigerians depend on the land for their living.

Until the 1970s, Nigeria was an exporter of food. During its boom years of the 1970s, however, the Nigerian government imported food. Importing food undermined farming in the country because the imported foods were often less expensive than locally produced foods. People moved from the rural areas to the cities in search of jobs, and farming suffered. In 2004, agriculture accounted for only 20 percent of the total value of Nigeria's production, whereas oil accounted for as much as 70 percent.

Economic Data

- Gross National Income (GNI) in U.S.$: 42,983,790,000
- World rank by GNI: 55
- GNI per capita in U.S.$: 320
- World rank by GNI per capita: 179
- Economic growth: 11%

Source: World Bank

ECONOMIC STRUCTURE

Over 60 percent of Nigerians still live and work in farming villages. Most of them work the land, producing food crops for their own use and selling any surplus at markets. In addition to farming, many Nigerians have other jobs, such as producing crafts or doing repair work.

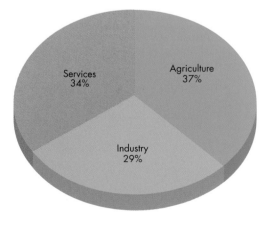

Services 34%

Agriculture 37%

Industry 29%

▲ Economy by sector

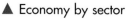

▲ This Nigerian woman works in the service sector, selling mobile phones.

In 1999, about 10 percent of Nigeria's workforce was involved in manufacturing industries, making products such as steel, pulp and paper, cloth and textiles, processed food, cement, and beer. Twenty percent worked in service industries, such as banking and transportation. Service industries are becoming more important in Nigeria, and in 2002, they accounted for 34 percent of the country's GDP. There has been some growth, particularly in banking and the civil service. Women are increasingly involved in Nigeria's job market, and a few Nigerian women are now qualifying as doctors, engineers, and bankers.

UNEMPLOYMENT

Unemployment has been a problem in Nigeria since the 1980s. It is difficult to calculate the exact number of people in the country without jobs. In 2000, however, it was estimated that sixty million were unemployed, mainly in the cities. In rural areas, people are given food and shelter by their families and are likely to be underemployed rather than unemployed. In other words, they have work but not enough to bring in a living wage.

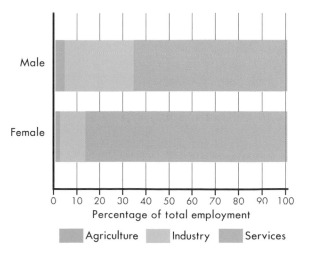

▲ Labor force by sector and gender

CHAPTER 8

Global Connections

For over seven hundred years, Nigeria has had strong links with other countries, mainly through trade. Nigeria's connections with the rest of the world have grown since it became independent in 1960.

◀ In 2004, Nigerian president Olusegun Obasanjo addressed the United Nations in New York.

NIGERIA AND AFRICA

Despite its difficulties at home, Nigeria has continued to play a prominent role in West Africa, where its relative wealth and large population make it the leading nation in the region. It was a founding member of the Economic Community of West African States (ECOWAS), which was established in 1975 to promote trade, cooperation, and self-reliance among West African states. Nigeria provided a peacekeeping force for the ECOWAS Ceasefire Monitoring Group (ECOMOG) when it contributed nine hundred personnel in August 1990 to serve in trouble spots throughout West Africa. In particular, Nigerian soldiers formed the basis of the ECOMOG peacekeeping force during the eleven-year war in Sierra Leone, which started in the early 1990s. Nigeria, however, had to withdraw its troops in 2000, because it could no longer afford the U.S. $1 million per day it was spending on peace enforcement in Sierra Leone.

NIGERIA'S ROLE IN THE WORLD

When it became independent in 1960, Nigeria joined the United Nations. The country also joined the Commonwealth, a voluntary association of fifty-three independent states that, apart from Mozambique, have directly or indirectly been under British rule, and Nigeria hosted the Heads of Commonwealth meeting in 2003. Along with South Africa, Nigeria is a leading voice within Africa. It condemned apartheid in South Africa and has argued for Africa to have a permanent place on the United Nations Security Council. Nigeria would like an African country such as itself, South Africa, or Egypt to join Britain, China, France, Russia, and the United States as a permanent member of the Security Council to ensure a better representation of African interests within the United Nations. The Security Council is the United Nations's most powerful body and works to maintain international peace.

Focus on: Nigeria, the African Union, and the Darfur Crisis

Nigeria plays a leading role in the African Union, the group that replaced the Organization of African Unity in 2002. The African Union aims to promote peace in Africa. In August 2004, Nigerian president Olusegun Obasanjo hosted talks to resolve the conflict in the Darfur region of Sudan, where civil war had led to the deaths of thousands of people. The Darfur revolt broke out in early 2003, after years of conflict between Arab nomads and African farmers over scarce resources in the arid, landlocked region. President Obasanjo urged the deployment of African Union forces to help restore peace in Sudan.

▼ Nigerian major-general Festus Okonkwo, chairman of the African Union mission in western Sudan's troubled Darfur region, inspects Rwandan troops in November 2004.

Nigeria has strategic importance as one of the world's major oil producers, and it is a member of the Organization of Petroleum Exporting Countries, which sets levels of output among its member states. OPEC influences the global supply—and, therefore, the price—of oil. Nigeria is the United States's second-biggest trading partner in Africa, after South Africa. The country is also a member of the World Trade Organization, which gives it the advantage of access to wider global markets.

▼ U.S. president George W. Bush stands with Nigerian president Olusegun Obasanjo at a summit in Abuja in 2003. This summit was held to consider closer economic ties between the United States and Nigeria and other African countries.

With its large population and the possibility that it may become more prosperous in the future, Nigeria could become a sizeable market for goods from other countries. The country could provide further trade opportunities for manufacturers and producers from North America, Europe, and the rest of Africa.

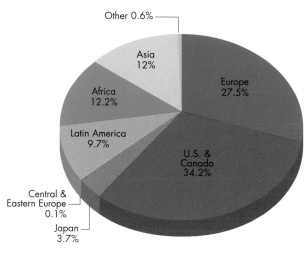

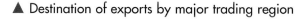
▲ Destination of exports by major trading region

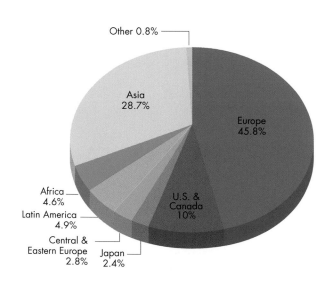
▲ Origin of imports by major trading region

NIGERIA AND THE ARTS

Nigeria's connections with the rest of the world extend beyond politics and economics. In particular, it has had a big influence in the arts. In the seventeenth and eighteenth centuries, Nigerian slaves carried their tradition of oral storytelling to the Caribbean, Latin America, and the United States, and Nigerian folktales and literature are known around the world. Particularly well known are the stories of Anancy the Spider. Nigeria's modern literature has been highly praised internationally, and Nigerians have won many awards. Nigerian novelist Wole Soyinka won the Nobel Prize for Literature in 1986. In 1991, Ben Okri, another Nigerian novelist, won the Booker Prize for *The Famished Road*.

The movement of people out of Nigeria has taken the influence of African music to many different parts of the world. African music was brought to the United States, Cuba, and Brazil by slaves, where it contributed to the development of jazz, blues, and modern popular music. Jazz is partly based on African techniques of interweaving rhythm and melody and call-and-response patterns. Calypso was heavily influenced by African work songs.

Did You Know?

Many early twentieth-century European artists, such as Pablo Picasso, Henri Matisse and Amedeo Modigliani, were influenced by wooden statues and masks from Nigeria.

▶ Traditional Nigerian masks like this one influenced some of the paintings of Pablo Picasso.

Focus on: The Nigerian Diaspora

Thousands of people have left Nigeria in search of work because the country's economic problems have led to a great deal of unemployment. At least 100,000 Nigerian professionals currently work in the United States. Britain, Canada, Saudi Arabia, and, increasingly, South Africa also have significant Nigerian communities. Since the 1970s, large-scale emigration from Nigeria is thought to have cost the country's economy about U.S.$100 billion.

CHAPTER 9

Transportation and Communications

Although Nigeria's transportation infrastructure was improved in the 1970s and 1980s, it has since fallen into disrepair. Its poor condition has had a harmful effect on businesses, which need to transport their goods around the country. When the new government took power in 1999, it decided to make improving transportation a priority.

ROAD AND RAIL

Poorly maintained roads are a particular problem during Nigeria's rainy season. Heavy downpours can create dangerous potholes in paved roads and sometimes even wash the roads away, making some rural areas inaccessible by car. When traveling both between and within cities, most Nigerians take buses or taxis. The use of motor scooters, motorcycles, and bicycles is common in northern Nigeria, where poverty is prevalent. In cities, many people travel in dilapidated, yellow, privately owned taxis, known as *danfos*, and overcrowded buses, known as *molues*. City roads

▼ Traffic congestion in Lagos.

are very congested, and Nigerians refer to traffic jams as "go-slows." Victoria Island, on which the central business district of Lagos is built and which has a bad reputation for traffic jams, is connected to the mainland by a bridge that is commonly known as the "crawl-over" because the traffic moves so slowly over it.

Nigeria's railroad network was built by the British primarily for transporting goods to ports for exporting. The country has about 2,210 miles (3,557 km) of railroad, but years of neglect have reduced the usefulness of both its rolling stock and its track. By 2004, for example, only about 15 percent of Nigeria's two hundred or so locomotives were in good working order. Concerned about the decline of what was once Africa's greatest railroad network, the Nigerian government announced a plan costing U.S.$60 billion to restore the country's railroads over the next twenty-five years. By February 2005, the first stages of this project were being set up to allow private companies to invest in and operate elements of the railroad system. It is hoped that private investment will help kick-start the project.

RIVER TRANSPORTATION

In the past—particularly during the colonial era—the Niger River was important for transporting freight. In the nineteenth century, British companies operated river vessels far inland. River transportation played a part in the growth of Nigeria's timber industry and in the establishment of palm and rubber plantations.

▲ Roads in Nigeria can often become impassable during the country's rainy season.

Transport & Communications Data

- 📁 Total roads:120,796 miles/194,394 km
- 📁 Total paved roads: 37,326 miles/60,068 km
- 📁 Total unpaved roads: 83,470 miles/ 134,326 km
- 📁 Total railways: 2,210 miles/3,557 km
- 📁 Major airports: 36
- 📁 Cars per 1,000 people: 8
- 📁 Cellular phones per 1,000 people: 26
- 📁 Personal computers per 1,000 people: 7
- 📁 Internet users per 1,000 people: 3

Sources: World Bank and CIA World Factbook

? Did You Know?

Nigeria has one of the highest road accident rates in the world. In Lagos, an average of one person is killed in a car accident each day.

Nigeria has over 1,875 miles (3,000 km) of potentially navigable inland waterways. In the late 1980s, a number of river ports were improved, and locks were constructed at the Kainji dam to allow ships to travel farther upstream. There has been renewed interest in river transportation because it is a cheap, safe, and environmentally friendly mode of transportation. In 1999, a project was started in the Lower Niger River to dredge and maintain a navigation channel of about 358 miles (576 km) from Baro to Warri.

MASS MEDIA COMMUNICATIONS

Successive Nigerian governments have claimed that they respect the freedom of the media. Nevertheless, journalists, broadcasters, and writers in Nigeria have been arrested and imprisoned for publishing stories that are critical of the government.

The Nigerian National Television Authority has thirty-two channels. It is the largest TV station in sub-Saharan Africa, based on the area that its broadcast signal reaches. Nigeria has nine privately owned TV stations. Muslim TV services started up in 2001 in northern Nigeria, broadcasting both religious and political programs. In September 2003, Nigeria launched its own satellite from Russia, which will eventually be used for communications. Nigerians who have satellite dishes or cable television often watch CNN; the BBC; and Movie Magic or Supersport, which are from South Africa.

Many Nigerians are newspaper readers. Most of the country's newspapers are published in English, but some are in local Nigerian languages, such as Yoruba and Hausa. Most of the radio stations in Nigeria are government-owned, and they broadcast in many different languages. Nigeria's international radio station—Voice of Nigeria—broadcasts across West Africa on short wave, and Nigerians also use Voice of America and the BBC World Service as sources of news. The country also has private radio stations, such as Cool FM.

◀ Newspapers are a very important source of information in a country where few people own TVs. Nigeria has an active press that publishes numerous national and regional papers.

THE RISE OF MOBILE PHONES

In 2001, licenses were granted to two cellular phone operators: MTN, from South Africa, and Econet, a multinational company now known as Vmobile. Nitel, a state-owned company, joined them in 2004. The introduction of cell phones has helped the millions of people who were frustrated by Nigeria's poor land lines.

Africa as a whole is the world's fastest-growing cellular phone market—increasing at a rate of 65 percent a year—and nowhere is it growing faster than in Nigeria, where the use of cellular phones has now outstripped use of land-line phones. In Nigeria, the number of cellular phone users soared from 37,000 in 2000 to about 3.3 million in early 2004.

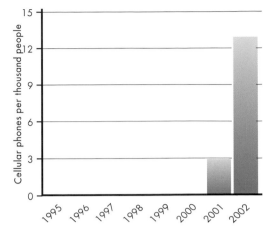

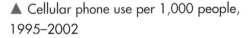

▲ Cellular phone use per 1,000 people, 1995–2002

Focus on: E-mail Scams

Internet cafés in Lagos are being used by criminals to send scam e-mails all over the world. The criminals pose as people who need to get money out of Nigeria and ask for an advance fee to help them do this. Many people in Britain, the United States, and elsewhere have fallen for these frauds. Nigeria's police are now locating and shutting down the Internet sites used by the scammers. In Nigeria, this type of crime is called a "419." This name refers to the section of the Criminal Code of Nigeria that makes it illegal.

▼ A billboard in Nigeria informs people that "419" Internet scams are illegal.

CHAPTER 10

Education and Health

Education is highly valued by most Nigerians, but educational standards in the country have fallen because of poverty and lack of government investment. The government does not provide any free schooling, so parents have to pay for their children's education.

SCHOOLS AND UNIVERSITIES

The policy that primary education is compulsory for children between the ages of six and eleven was introduced in Nigeria in the 1970s. This policy is hard for the government to enforce, however, because parents cannot always afford to send their children to school. In Nigerian communities, it is considered more important to educate boys than girls because boys are expected to become breadwinners. Girls are usually the first to be removed from school if money is short in their families. This is particularly true in Muslim areas, where little value is placed on girls having a formal education. This is reflected in the fact that literacy rates for women in the north are about 20 percent lower than for women in the south.

Education and Health Data

- Life expectancy at birth, male: 48
- Life expectancy at birth, female: 49.6
- Infant mortality rate per 1,000: 110
- Under-five mortality rate per 1,000: 183
- Physicians per 1,000 people: 0.3
- Health expenditure as % of GDP: 3.0%
- Education expenditure as % of GDP: 0.9%
- Primary school net enrollment: 56%
- Student-teacher ratio, primary: 40
- Adult literacy as % age 15+: 66.8

Sources: United Nations Agencies and World Bank

◀ Nigeria's culture values education of boys more highly than education of girls.

Children must pass the common entrance exam in order to go to secondary school. Only about 23 percent of Nigeria's children attend secondary school. Secondary-school students take the senior secondary school exam at the end of their last year, after which they may go to universities and colleges for higher education. Nigeria has about forty universities and twenty-seven technical colleges. Many Nigerians prefer to go to the United States or Britain to study because degrees from foreign universities are valued by Nigerian employers.

EDUCATION SYSTEMS

European-style education was introduced to Nigeria by Christian missionaries in the 1840s. Children in the country's primary schools are usually taught in English and sometimes also in a local language. In Islamic communities, children attend religious schools called *madrassahs*, in which they study Arabic and memorize sections of the Qur'an. Students at these religious schools also study subjects taught in European-style schools.

In many rural areas, children are educated informally by working alongside their parents, by becoming apprentices, or by participating in community life. They learn a trade, such as farming or carpentry, and traditional crafts, such as leatherwork. They are also

▲ This boy studies in a madrassah near Kano, in northern Nigeria. Madrassahs offer education based on Islamic teachings. In Nigeria, they are most commonly found in the north of the country, where Islam is the dominant religion.

educated about cultural traditions, survival skills, and social activities. Children often receive this informal education alongside more formal Muslim or European-style schooling. A few children only get informal education.

Nigeria has a tradition of "fostering," in which parents send a child to live with a family in an urban center or another country for the child to attend school. Families will often make great sacrifices in order to do this, in the hope that a better education will allow their child to get a well-paid job and help support the family.

? Did You Know?

Educated Nigerians often speak English, as well as one or two of Nigeria's four hundred native languages, such as Yoruba, Hausa, or Igbo.

POVERTY AND POOR HEALTH

Those Nigerians who can afford to pay for health care have access to very good, but expensive, private hospitals and clinics. For most of the country's people, however, medical facilities, supplies, equipment, and staff are in short supply. Part of the reason for this is that many Nigerian doctors and nurses leave the country to find higher-paid work overseas.

The infant mortality rate in Nigeria—which was 110 per 1,000 live births in 2002—is one of the highest in the world. Common causes of infant mortality include diarrhea, acute respiratory infections, measles, and malaria. All of these diseases are preventable.

Nigeria has a relatively high rate of diabetes; about 2 percent of the population has the disease. The incidence of sickle cell anemia, a hereditary disease occurring mostly in those of

▼ Life expectancy at birth, 1960–2002

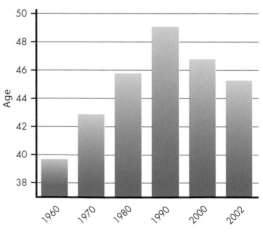

◀ Lack of basic services, especially lack of access to water, has a big impact on health in Nigeria. Many Nigerians have no running water and are forced to buy their water in plastic containers like the ones being sold here.

African descent, is also high. Other common diseases are tuberculosis, malaria, and polio.

There is often a direct connection between ill-health and poverty. Nigeria's government has set goals for improving health care in the country, but it has a long way to go before meeting them. Nigeria's total health spending in 2001 was 3.4 percent of the country's GDP. In the same year, the United States spent 13.9 percent of its GDP on health care, and in Britain the figure was 7.6 percent of GDP. According to the World Health Organization (WHO), Nigeria's health-care system ranked among the world's worst. Out of 190 countries ranked in 2000, Nigeria was 187th on the list.

HIV/AIDS

Many cases of HIV/AIDS go unreported in Nigeria because of the stigma attached to the disease. It is estimated, however, that over 170,000 deaths in the country in 2001 were attributable to AIDS. The stigma surrounding HIV/AIDS has made it difficult to educate people about the causes of the disease. Nigeria has few places where individuals can get tested for HIV/AIDS, and antiretroviral drugs are too expensive for most Nigerians who suffer from the disease. In 2004, the country already had one million AIDS orphans and over four million people thought to be infected with HIV. This figure is expected to double by 2010.

? Did You Know?

In 2004, a new plant for manufacturing anti-retroviral drugs opened in Lagos. This facility was set up and funded by Nigerian health professionals working in the United States, and it aims to provide affordable treatment for those with HIV/AIDS.

◄Posters put up by Nigeria's government warn people about the dangers of HIV/AIDS and tell them how to avoid infection.

Focus on: Polio Immunization

In 2003, a polio immunization campaign was stopped in northern Nigeria because Islamic leaders in Kano spread a false rumor that the vaccines were contaminated with antifertility drugs as part of a U.S. plot to stop Muslim women from having children. As a result of the stop of polio immunizations in the area, the Global Polio Eradication Initiative traced new outbreaks of polio to the Kano area. Other African nations, including Mali and Guinea, that had been free of polio, also suffered polio outbreaks linked to those in Kano. In August 2004, using supplies from Islamic countries, polio vaccinations were restarted in northern Nigeria to bring the outbreak under control.

CHAPTER 11

Culture and Religion

In a country with so many different ethnic groups, some people think it is more accurate to talk of Nigeria's many different cultures rather than a single national culture. In reality, however, Nigeria's many ethnic groups share many cultural beliefs and practices.

For example, the performing arts—especially storytelling, plays, and dance—have an important role in Nigerian culture. Such performances are often associated with cultural and religious holidays and family events, such as weddings and naming ceremonies. Extended family members attend these functions, which usually include a lavish feast with as much food as the hosts can afford and music for dancing. Special music is played for different occasions, and these celebrations can go on for several days.

FAMILY LIFE

Extended families are the norm in Nigeria, particularly in rural areas. Parents, children, grandchildren, and other relatives usually all live close to each other in a compound or under one roof. In urban areas, smaller, nuclear families are becoming more common, but they still maintain strong links with their extended families and frequently visit them or receive visits from them. Nigerians have a strong sense of responsibility toward their families and their communities. In a country that has no state support for the elderly, younger family members usually care for elderly relatives. In some urban areas, however, this practice is less common today than it was in the past.

Women in Muslim communities, especially those in northern Nigeria, are often kept in seclusion and are not permitted even to leave the home. They do all the domestic work, such as cooking, cleaning, and caring for children. But in other parts of Nigeria, particularly in towns and cities, women are starting to lead more independent lives, and they are increasingly going out to work. Although many Muslim women's lives remain restricted, some are even getting involved in Nigerian politics. These women, however, often encounter opposition from some men and from some religious leaders.

▶ Life is changing for some Nigerian women. These women in Jigawa are training to become tailors and learning to run their own businesses. Many Nigerian women, however, are victims of domestic violence.

FOOD

What Nigerians eat depends on whether they live in urban or rural areas, whether they live in the north or the south of the country, and what religion they follow. In the north, the usual diet is based on grains eaten with spicy vegetable sauces or a kind of kebab known as *tsire*. Muslims do not eat pork or drink alcohol. In the south, root crops such as yams and cassava are a staple and are eaten with spicy, peppery stews and sauces. Fish is an important part of the Nigerian diet, except in the north, where goat is more commonly eaten. Fish is preserved by smoking or drying. Snack foods, which can be bought from roadside stalls, include fried yam chips, meat pastries, and doughnuts.

RELIGIOUS BELIEFS

The majority of Nigeria's Christians are found in the southern regions of the country, although a few live in the north. Most of the Yoruba people are Protestants and Anglicans. The Igbo, in contrast, are mainly Catholics. Christianity was introduced to Nigeria by missionaries during the colonial period. In Yorubaland, in the southwest, evangelical and charismatic African churches have been founded, breaking away from the European-based form of Christianity. These churches have introduced African music and dance into their services.

▼ A large congregation crowds into an evangelical Pentacostal Christian church in Lagos.

▲ These Nigerian Muslims observe Friday prayers at a rural mosque in Kano.

About half the people of Nigeria are Muslim. The Hausa and Fulani peoples in the north are predominantly Muslim, and a significant number of Yorubas are also Muslim. Daily prayers, attending a mosque, reading the Qur'an, and following Islamic law are major elements of the Islamic faith. Every Muslim hopes to go on the hajj, a pilgrimage to Mecca, in Saudi Arabia, at least once in his or her life.

? Did You Know?

Nigeria's film industry, known as Nollywood, began in the 1970s. By 2004, it had become the third-largest film industry in the world. Nollywood produces over two thousand low-budget films per year and distributes them on video all over Africa, where they are hugely popular.

During the month of Ramadan, which is the ninth month of the year in the Muslim calendar, Muslims fast during daylight hours. Ramadan is followed by the feast of *Eid-al-Fitr*.

Traditional religions exist alongside Islam and Christianity. Followers of traditional religions often also pray to the Islamic God (Allah) and

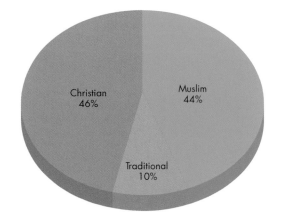

Christian
46%

Muslim
44%

Traditional
10%

▲ Major religions as percentage of total population

the Christian God, along with their own gods and ancestral spirits. Followers of traditional Nigerian religions believe in gods that live in natural elements such as rain and thunder. They also offer gifts such as food to the spirits of their ancestors in return for help with their daily lives. For people who believe in ancestral spirits, a Nigerian funeral is an occasion for celebration, because the person who has died is joining his or her ancestors.

▶ A traditional Nigerian religious practitioner, or juju man, in Benin City, sits with pots, candles, and other objects that he uses to perform rituals.

? Did You Know?

According to a survey conducted by the BBC in 2004, Nigeria is the most religious nation in the world. Over 90 percent of Nigerians said they believed in a god, prayed regularly, and would die for their religious beliefs.

Focus on: Masks and Masquerades

Masquerades are important rituals in many traditional religions in Nigeria, particularly among the Igbo people. According to Nigerian traditional religions, people are immortal, and through the use of masks and masquerades, dead ancestors can visit the land of the living. Most masquerades involve dancing and singing, but they vary from one community to another. Costumes are made of grass, palm fronds, cloth, or raffia, and masks are made from carved wood. Women, except those past childbearing age, are usually excluded from masquerades.

▶ A masquerade in Badagry, west of Lagos. The masquerade performers often dance in the street and ask their audience for money.

CHAPTER 12

Leisure and Tourism

The idea of structured leisure time is a new one in Nigeria. People in all communities have always found time, for example, to spend with family members and friends, talking about their lives or celebrating a birth. In Nigeria's cities, however, life is changing fast, and people spend more time taking part in activities and outings, such as visiting museums and parks, going to clubs, and attending concerts.

LEISURE TIME IN RURAL AREAS

Nigerians in rural areas enjoy different leisure activities, especially festivals. For example, regattas are very popular on the rivers, and there are festivals dedicated to crops and livestock, such as the Yam Festival in the southeast and the Crops Festival in Kaduna.

NATIONAL HOLIDAYS

The religious festivals of Nigeria's two main religions—Good Friday, Easter Monday, Christmas Day, and Boxing Day for Christians, and *Eid-al-Fitr*, *Eid-al-Kabir*, and *Eid-al-Maulud* for Muslims—are observed as national holidays by all Nigerians. People who have moved to the cities often return to their home

▼ Young men drumming, singing, and dancing on the beach.

villages for these occasions to spend them with other family members.

URBAN NIGHTLIFE AND MUSIC

In the cities, young people who can afford entertainment flock to movie theaters and nightclubs. People dance through the night and listen to a wide range of music styles, from juju and apala to highlife—a fusion of western and African music—and makossa. Juju has a similar heavy beat to reggae. It started out as a style known as "palm wine music," that used banjos, guitars, shakers, and hand drums. Juju groups today use more percussion instruments, as well as electric guitars, and this type of music is now internationally famous. Popular juju-music stars include King Sunny Ade and Chief Commander Ebenezer Obey.

GAMES

Across Nigeria, people play a game known by the Yoruba as *ayo* and by the Hausa as *dara*. Using a board and seeds or stones, two players try to capture their opponents' seeds by landing in the same space. Young boys enjoy playing marbles, while girls prefer skipping and clapping games involving rhythm and singing. Nigerian children often make their own toys out of recycled materials. They may, for example, make a soccer ball from plastic bags and rubber bands or a top from a coconut.

? Did You Know?

Famous Nigerian soccer player Taribo West has an unusual background for a World Cup player. Having grown up as a juvenile street-gang member in one of the toughest districts of Lagos, he now preaches as a Christian pastor when he isn't playing soccer.

▼ Boys play soccer in Kaduna, in northern Nigeria.

SPORTS

Nigerians excel at sport of all kinds. Soccer is by far the most popular sport in the country. In the 1996 Olympic Games, the Super Eagles, Nigeria's national soccer team, won the gold medal. Several Nigerian soccer players, including Peter Odemwingie and Victor Ikpeda, have moved to Europe, where they receive high salaries. Nigerians have also excelled at an international level in track events and boxing. Their team won the bronze medal in both the 4-by-100 meter and 4-by-400 meter relays at the 2004 Olympics in Athens. The Nigerian boxer Mudeen Ganiyu made it to the quarter-finals in the 2004 Olympics. No Nigerian boxer, however, has ever won an Olympic gold medal, even though the Nigerian government offered a prize of U.S. $10,000 to any of its boxers who won a gold medal in 2004.

Among the Yoruba, traditional wrestling is very popular. Nigeria has several different kinds of traditional wrestling, such as *iga kadi*, which is like a free-for-all with very few rules, and *eke,* which has its own special techniques and rules. Traditional African games existed before colonists came to Nigeria, and Nigerians are eager to preserve them.

TOURISM

Nigeria's turbulent past has prevented it from becoming a popular tourist destination. Potential visitors have been put off by periodic violence, high crime rates, poor infrastructure, and the general disorganization of the country. With its vibrant culture and numerous artistic and natural attractions, however, Nigeria has

▼ Joan Elcah, a member of the Nigerian Olympic team, trains before the 2004 Olympics.

great potential for tourism. It has good beaches, such as those at Lekki near Lagos; dramatic scenery in the Eastern Highlands and around Jos; and a rich cultural mix of Arabic and European musical and architectural influences in places like Kano. It also has a thriving arts-and-crafts scene and is well known for textiles and pottery. As a degree of stability has returned to Nigeria in recent years, the number of tourists has slowly been increasing. The Nigerian government is eager to develop the tourist industry and sees it as one way of reducing the country's dependence on oil.

Tourism in Nigeria Data

- Tourist arrivals, millions: 0.831
- Earnings from tourism in U.S.$: 156,000,000
- Tourism as % foreign earnings: 1
- Tourist departures, millions: not available
- Expenditure on tourism in U.S.$: 700,000,000

Source: World Bank

▲ Wikki Warm Springs, in Yankari National Park, in central Nigeria, is a potential tourist destination.

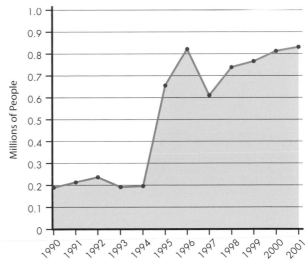

▲ Changes in international tourist arrivals, 1990–2001

Focus on: New Opportunities for Tourism

In 2004, Nigeria's tourist industry was very small, but the country's government is targeting people interested in the environment and African Americans interested in their heritage as possible tourists. Ecotourism, such as bird-watching trips, and heritage tourism, which involves trips to ancient sites, offer exciting opportunities for Nigeria's developing tourist industry. The old slave-trading town of Badagry, with its Museum of Slave Trade and early missionaries' cemeteries, is being developed as a tourist attraction. The ancient walled cities in the north, with their Islamic architecture and colorful markets, could also attract visitors in the future.

CHAPTER 13

Environment and Conservation

Nigeria's natural environment is under considerable stress from the country's growing population, poverty, and the effects of people's actions, such as the cutting down of trees. As a result of these problems, Nigeria's environment may eventually become unable to support its people, and poverty will increase.

DEFORESTATION AND LAND DEGRADATION

For hundreds of years, people have been cutting down Nigeria's trees to clear space for farming or to obtain building materials and fuel. Nigeria originally had forest cover of about 27,800 sq miles (72,000 sq km). By 2004, this was down to 3,860 sq miles (10,000 sq km), and the country's forests still are being cleared at the rate of about 14 percent a year. Recent depletion is the result of road building and the clearing of land for farms and pastures, as well as logging. Much of the logging is illegal.

The lack of vegetation, the removal of trees that hold the soil in place, and heavy rainfall have led to particularly bad soil erosion in Nigeria, especially on the Jos Plateau, where there is a high density of population and poor soil. In the north, deforestation, irrigation, and over-grazing are leading to land degradation and desertification, or the process by which land turns into desert. These processes threaten to destroy rare plant and animal species and render the land useless for farming.

▼ Soil erosion, shown here in the Jos Plateau region, is caused by the removal of vegetation.

Environmental and Conservation Data

📂 Forested area as % total land area: 2

📂 Protected area as % total land area: 6

📂 Number of protected areas: 1,009

SPECIES DIVERSITY

Category	Known species (1992–2002)	Threatened species
Mammals	274	27
Breeding birds	286	9
Reptiles	154	2
Amphibians	53	not available
Fish	95	2
Plants	4,715	119

Source: World Resources Institute

URBAN POLLUTION

Many Nigerian cities suffer from polluted water supplies, bad sanitation, and inadequate sewage systems. In addition, heavy traffic and poorly maintained vehicles produce a large amount of air pollution. Pollutants that contaminate air, water, and soil resources are also generated by industries that are often poorly regulated. In Kano, for example, pollution from slaughterhouses, tanneries, and factories seriously threatens the quantity and quality of local water resources. Furthermore, because of the Kano region's low and unreliable rainfall, toxic elements that accumulate in its water systems are not flushed away regularly by the flow of water. Instead, the toxins become concentrated, and contaminate the water sources. Nigeria's government is now intervening to reduce pollution. For example, it has banned the importing of vehicles over five years old in order to cut the number of polluting vehicles on Nigeria's roads.

▶ In the absence of a waste-collection service, some people in Nigeria dump their garbage alongside city streets such as this one on the outskirts of Kano.

WILDLIFE

In the early twentieth century, Nigeria was still home to elephants, buffalo, lions, and leopards. Many of these animals have now disappeared because people hunted them for their meat. In addition, their habitats have been destroyed by urbanization, deforestation, land clearance, road building, and other human activities. Nigeria's endangered species are found only in major reserves, zoos, or very remote areas. Much of Nigeria's other wildlife is seriously threatened. About 10 percent of mammal species and 3 percent of bird species, for example, are threatened with extinction.

▲ A child goes home to a shack on Bonny Island in the Niger Delta. Many people in this part of Nigeria live in similarly harsh conditions.

Focus on: Oil Pollution in the Niger Delta

The exploitation of its oil resources has had a devastating effect on the Niger Delta. The land has been subjected to oil spills, and the groundwater has been polluted. Much of the pollution is a result of people breaking into oil pipelines to steal oil to sell on the black market. In 2004, the Nigerian government reported that thefts from oil pipelines added up to 145,000 barrels per day, an amount worth about U.S. $2 billion a year. Oil pollution has badly affected the Delta region's fragile forests and mangrove swamps and has had a disastrous impact on the people there, many of whom make their livings from farming and fishing.

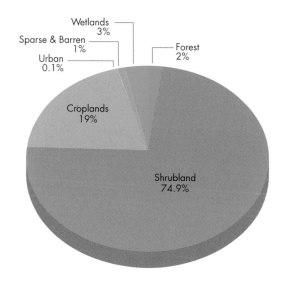

▲ Habitat type as percentage of total area

WHAT IS BEING DONE?

Among Nigeria's more than one thousand protected areas are twelve game and forest reserves and eight national parks, where wildlife is protected. The Omo Forest Reserve, 84 miles (135 km) northeast of Lagos, has African forest elephants, chimpanzees, and other endangered species. In this reserve, researchers and environmentalists carry out scientific studies of the wildlife and try to prevent poaching and illegal logging. Also, many traditional farming practices that are still being used, such as planting trees and hedgerows, terracing steep slopes, and applying manure, are now being recognized as sustainable ways of farming, conserving, and managing the land.

Nigeria's Federal Environmental Protection Agency was established in 1988, but so far, it has had little impact. The government's plan to end gas flaring by 2008, however, will not only reduce greenhouse gas emissions, but will also provide both more gas for domestic consumption and more gas for export via the West Africa Gas Pipeline. Nigeria also cooperates with its neighbors, Cameroon, Chad, and Niger, in the management of wildlife in the Chad Basin. Many conservation groups, such as the World Wide Fund for Nature, are working to try to ensure that Nigeria's government protects the environment. These groups also work to force oil companies to prevent oil leaks.

▼ Giraffes roam in Yankari National Park.

Focus on: Nigeria's Rain Forest

About 95 percent of Nigeria's original tropical rain forest, most of it in Cross River, has been destroyed. Nigeria's government has now made logging illegal in this area. This is a critical step in protecting one of West Africa's last remaining tropical forests. Cross River's forests still contain gorillas, chimpanzees, forest elephants, and the highly endangered drill monkey. These forests also protect the watershed on which more than three hundred rural communities depend.

Focus on: Gray Parrots

Conservationists are increasingly concerned about the growing trade in gray parrots. According to the Convention on International Trade in Endangered Species (CITES), only limited trade in these birds is allowed under strict licensing. It is estimated, however, that each year between five thousand and ten thousand gray parrots are smuggled out of forests in eastern Nigeria and sold in Asia and the Middle East. These parrots are popular because they are able to mimic human speech.

CHAPTER 14

Future Challenges

Some people claim that Nigeria is not a developing nation but, rather, an "undeveloping" nation. Its people are actually much worse off now than they were in the 1960s. The World Bank ranks Nigeria as the thirteenth-poorest country in the world, with 60 percent of its population living below the poverty line, in spite of its huge potential for wealth based on its oil and other resources.

POVERTY

There is an enormous gap between the rich and the poor in Nigeria. According to a 2004 World Bank report, about 80 percent of Nigeria's oil and natural gas revenues goes to just 1 percent of the country's population. This combination of poverty for the vast majority, and wealth for a small minority, has made many people feel desperate and resentful, and it has often led to unrest in the country. With a stable, civilian government that is more answerable to the people, Nigerians hope that the potential wealth, energy, and talent that exist in Nigeria could lead to a country that is self-reliant and prosperous and in which income from natural resources is invested more equally and sustainably.

▼ Barefoot children beg for money outside a supermarket and Internet café used by richer Nigerians. Great inequality exists in many of Nigeria's urban centers.

▲ Local health clinics, such as this one near Kano, play a crucial role in the fight against HIV/AIDS.

HIV/AIDS

Whatever progress Nigeria's government is able to make in developing its economy and stabilizing its society will be undermined if it is not able to stop the increase in HIV/AIDS infection. The National Intelligence Council in the United States has identified Nigeria as one of the five countries that is facing a drastic increase in HIV/AIDS, and this crisis puts severe strain on its government's resources.

Nigeria has been slow to confront the HIV/AIDS epidemic. The government is now taking action by training health workers, providing preventive counseling, and expanding AIDS testing facilities, and it is appealing for U.S. $248 million in aid to help it provide subsidized antiretroviral drugs for people living with HIV/AIDS. Nigeria needs help from the World Health Organization and other countries in its fight against AIDS.

NATIONAL UNITY

The government of Nigeria has the challenge of reconciling the demands of the country's diverse ethnic and religious groups. Major tensions continue to exist over access to resources. This has led some people to wonder whether Nigeria should remain as one country, as originally created by British colonizers, or break apart into several separate states. The experience of the Biafra War is still vivid in the minds of many Nigerians and affects their thinking. A survey in 2001 found that most Nigerians wanted the nation to remain intact. Only one person out of five thought that the differences between Nigerians were too strong to overcome and that the country should be divided.

Time Line

9000 B.C. Earliest evidence of human habitation in Nigeria.

500 B.C.–A.D. 200 Nok culture flourishes.

A.D. 900 Emergence of kingdom of Kanem around Lake Chad, and establishment of the Igbo civilization.

1100 Establishment of Yoruba city-states.

Late 1400s Arrival of Portuguese traders.

1500 Peak of the Benin kingdom.

1804 Muslim holy wars (jihads) against the Hausa and Yoruba city-states.

1807 Britain outlaws the slave trade.

1861 Lagos is annexed by the British.

1884 Berlin Conference in which Africa is divided up between European powers.

1886 The Yoruba wars end.

1990 Declaration of Nigeria as two protectorates.

1914 Unification of Nigeria into one state.

1950s Discovery of oil in Nigeria.

1960 Nigeria gains its independence from Britain.

1963 Nigeria becomes a federal republic.

1966 A military regime takes over Nigeria.

1967–1970 Biafra War.

1971 Nigeria joins OPEC.

1976 Nigerian capital is moved from Lagos to Abuja.

1979–1983 A brief period of civilian rule in Nigeria.

1986 Wole Soyinka wins Nobel Prize for Literature.

1991 Ben Okri wins Britain's Booker Prize for his novel, *The Famished Road.*

1991 Census held in Nigeria.

1996 Nigeria's soccer team wins the Olympic gold medal.

1999 Nigeria returns to civilian democratic rule.

2000 Declaration of Sharia (Islamic law) in several northern Nigerian states.

2002 Establishment of the African Union.

2003 Nigeria launches its own satellite from Russia.

Glossary

annex (of a country or state) to take control of another country or state

antiretroviral drugs medicines used to treat HIV/AIDS

apartheid a system of government introduced in South Africa in 1948 to keep black, white, mixed-race, and Asian people separate and unequal

autonomous rule self-government by a state or group of people

calabash a large, hard fruit with a shell that can be dried and used as a bowl

city-state a city which, with the surrounding country area, forms an independent state

civilian government a nonmilitary, democratically elected government, made up of representatives

coup a sudden, often violent, takeover of a government

delta an area of low, fertile land where a river divides into branches toward the sea

diabetes a disease in which too much urine is excreted and blood-sugar levels are too high

Economic Community of West African States (ECOWAS) a regional group of sixteen West African countries, founded in 1975

ecotourism tourism that minimizes damage to sites visited for their natural or cultural value

equatorial very hot as a result of being near the equator

evangelical/charismatic churches certain fundamentalist Protestant Christian churches that place particular emphasis on the importance of faith, studying the Bible, and public preaching

federal capital the capital of a country as a whole, as opposed to the capital of a state within that country

global warming the warming of Earth's surface as a result of gases trapping heat in the planet's atmosphere

gross domestic product (GDP) the total market value of all goods and services produced in a country

gross national income (GNI) a country's gross domestic product plus the net income it earns from investments in other countries in a given year; also called gross national product (GNP)

HIV/AIDS human immunodeficiency virus (HIV) is a virus spread by unprotected sex or contaminated needles or blood supplies that can develop into acquired immunodeficiency syndrome (AIDS), which is a fatal disease

human rights the nonpolitical rights that belong to any person without regard of race, religion, color, or sex

infant mortality the number of babies, out of every one thousand born, who die before the age of one

infrastructure the basic system of public works in a country, state, or region, such as roads, railroads, electricity, and phone lines necessary for a society to function

malaria a tropical disease transmitted to people through mosquito bites

mangrove a semisubmerged tropical forest found in coastal regions of the tropics

palm oil the oil from the nut of an African palm tree that is widely used in West African cooking

protectorate a country controlled and protected by a more powerful nation that takes charge, in particular, of its defense and foreign affairs

sedimentary made from bits of rock and soil that have been gathered, moved around, and then left in a place by water or ice

semiarid receiving less than 4 to 24 inches (10 to 61 cm) of rain per year

tuberculosis an infectious disease that attacks the lungs and may spread to other organs

watershed an area bounded by a divide and draining into particular body of water

Further Information

BOOKS TO READ

*Bound for America: The Forced Migration
of Africans to the New World*
James Haskins
(HarperCollins)

*A Good Soup Attracts Chairs: A First
African Cookbook for American Kids*
Fran Osseo-Asare
(Pelican)

Hausaland Tales from the Nigerian Marketplace
Gavin McIntosh
(Linnet Books)

Life in Ancient Africa
(Peoples of the Ancient World series)
Hazel Richardson
(Crabtree)

Nigeria (Africa series)
Ida Walker
(Mason Crest)

Nigeria (Changing Face of series)
Rob Bowden
(Raintree)

Nigeria (Countries of the World series)
Yinka Ismail
(Gareth Stevens)

*Nigeria: 1880 To the Present: The Struggle, the
Tragedy, the Promise (Exploration of Africa: the
Emerging Nations* series)
Daniel E. Harmon
(Chelsea House)

The Slave Trade (Events & Outcomes series)
Tom Monaghan
Raintree

USEFUL WEB SITES

Art and Life in Africa
www.uiowa.edu/~africart/toc/people.html

Embassy of the Federal Republic of Nigeria
www.nigeriaembassyusa.org

Hopes on the Horizon
www.pbs.org/hopes/nigeria/index.html

Map of Nigeria
www.lib.utexas.edu/maps/africa/nigeria.gif

Nigeria Art
www.nigeria-arts.net/

The Nigeria Congress
www.nigeriacongress.org/

Nigerian Recipes
www.onlinenigeria.com/recipes/recipes.asp

World Almanac for Kids: Nigeria
www.worldalmanacforkids.com/explore/
nations/nigeria.html

Index